Gift
489

Mary Guttirrz
C E E

SULEIMAN
THE
ELEPHANT

Never before seen in Germany,
This elephant was here
On the second of January.

(INN SIGN, BRIXEN)

When King Max to Salzburg came
He had an elephant in tow.
So big and tall his giant frame,
He looked in every window.
Thus evermore this house has been
Known to all as The Elephant Inn.

(INN SIGN, SALZBURG)

Elephant is this animal's name.
His shape is painted on this wall
To show his looks to one and all,
How he with King Maximilian came
On the long journey home from Spain.

(INN SIGN, AUER)

Copyright © 1984 by Margret Rettich.
First published in the Federal Republic of Germany by Otto Maier Verlag in 1984.
Translation copyright © 1986 by Elizabeth D. Crawford.
Printed in the United States of America.
First U.S. Edition 1986.

1 2 3 4 5 6 7 8 9 10

Library of Congress Cataloging in Publication Data
Rettich, Margret.   Suleiman the elephant.
Translation of: Soliman der Elefant.
Summary: Follows Maximilian, son of King Ferdinand of Austria, and his wedding present, the elephant Suleiman, in their procession from Spain to Vienna in 1551. 1. Soliman (Elephant)—Juvenile literature. 2. Maximilian II, Emperor of Germany, 1527–1576—Juvenile literature. 3. Austria—Kings and rulers—Biography—Juvenile literature. 4. Holy Roman Empire—Kings and rulers—Biography—Juvenile literature. [1. Soliman (Elephant) 2. Elephants. 3. Maximilian II, Emperor of Germany, 1527–1576] I. Title. DB65.4.R4713 1986   943′.029′0924 [B]   86-2737
ISBN 0-688-05741-1
ISBN 0-688-05742-X (lib. ed.)

MARGRET RETTICH

SULEIMAN THE ELEPHANT

TRANSLATED FROM THE GERMAN BY ELIZABETH D. CRAWFORD

This is the story of Suleiman the elephant.
In 1551 he journeyed from Spain
through Italy, the Tyrol, and Austria, to Vienna.
Today there are many inns called The Elephant
along the road he traveled.

LOTHROP, LEE, & SHEPARD BOOKS
NEW YORK

Once upon a time there was a prince named Max, who lived in Austria. His father was King Ferdinand the First.

In those days a prince had to marry a princess, so when Prince Max was a small child, he was betrothed to Princess Maria. But he had never seen her.

Princess Maria lived far, far away, in Spain. Her father was Emperor Charles the Fifth.

I hope I like Prince Max, Maria would think sometimes.

And Max would think, What if I don't like Princess Maria at all? They were both just a little bit anxious.

At last the time came when Princess Maria and Prince Max were old enough to marry. Emperor Charles announced the wedding. It was to be a magnificent affair. Everyone who was anyone was to be there. Kings and princes, dukes and cardinals, and their followers were traveling all the way to Spain.

King Ferdinand, Max's father, was the only one who sent his regrets. He had a very serious worry. At that time the Turks were besieging his capital city of Vienna. The leader of the Turks, Suleiman, was a very dangerous fellow. He had boasted that he would first conquer the city and then plunder it and burn it to the ground. The Viennese were very much afraid, and so King Ferdinand simply could not leave them alone, even for his son's wedding.

Prince Max would rather have stayed in Vienna too, but after all, he was the bridegroom, so he had to go to the wedding.

"Courage!" he cried as he left. "I'll be back soon, and together we'll drive away the Turks."

Then he waved once more and went on his way.

Meanwhile, in the imperial palace in Spain, everything was being readied for the wedding. Colored banners fluttered from the towers. Garlands of flowers hung everywhere. The cellars were bulging with countless barrels of wine. Roast oxen turned on the spits. Pans sizzled, pots bubbled, kettles simmered. There was a wonderful smell of roasting and baking.

One after the other, the important guests arrived, bringing costly presents. Finally Prince Max was the only one missing, and everyone awaited him eagerly.

Emperor Charles sat on a throne under a canopy. Beside him sat Princess Maria in her most beautiful dress. She was very excited. At last she and Max would see each other for the first time.

Then Max came riding into the castle courtyard. He looked about him, but he never saw Maria at all. He only had eyes for the present from the king of Portugal.

The king's present was a gigantic animal. It was as high as a house. It had legs like columns, ears like sails, and a hide like the wall of a fortress. But the most remarkable thing about it was a long, thick snake at the front of its head.

"W-w-what kind of an animal is that?" Max stammered in astonishment.

The king of Portugal was delighted that his present had made such an impression, for he loved to show that he was just as rich and powerful as Emperor Charles. At that time he ruled over India, half of Africa, and half of America. "This animal is an elephant," he answered. "He comes from India, which belongs to me. The elephant belongs to you."

Max fell out of his saddle for pure joy. He ran around the elephant and even dared to touch him. The elephant swept Max's hat off his head with his trunk.

Max never glanced at Maria. She could have wept, but instead she smiled, for she had been taught that a Spanish princess never shows disappointment or sadness.

The next day the marriage took place. Afterward there was a
banquet. Servants brought out one course after another, and Max
gave his elephant a big mouthful from each dish to taste.

Then Max climbed onto a chair and made an announcement.
"This elephant shall be called Suleiman!" he shouted.

"Oho!" said the guests. They knew that Suleiman was the name
of the Turkish leader who was besieging Vienna.

"With my elephant Suleiman," Max cried, "I will chase away
Suleiman the Turk, and all the other Turks, too. Then my elephant
will be a hero, and my father, King Ferdinand, will make him a
knight. A toast to Sir Suleiman Elephant!"

And then Max tumbled down in a heap, for he had had too much Spanish wine to drink. A few courtiers dragged him away, joking to each other, "Prince Max didn't marry our Princess Maria today—he's gotten himself married to an elephant!"

When the eating was finished, the music struck up for dancing. The guests enjoyed themselves until late into the night.

Charles the Fifth sat there looking thunderous. He was angry about the king of Portugal and his present.

Princess Maria sat beside him and smiled. But later, when she was all alone, she wept.

After the wedding Max wanted to hasten back to Vienna. It was autumn, and soon winter would come. If they didn't hurry, they would run into snow and ice, and that would not be good for the elephant.

Maria had to make her farewells. She was leaving behind everything she cared about: her goldfish, her tame birds, and her kind old nurse. She took only her clothes and her wedding presents.

They set off with a fleet of many ships. On the sixth day they were attacked by pirates. These sea robbers hated the Emperor Charles, so they planned to steal his daughter and sell her to Suleiman, the leader of the Turks. As they were fighting, suddenly the elephant burst out of his shed and trumpeted. The pirates stared at him in horror. Then they fled. Maria was safe.

But they had captured one ship, and as luck would have it, it was the one carrying Maria's clothes and the wedding presents. "Never mind," said Max. "Everyone could see that my elephant is a hero. He drove off the pirates all by himself—just the way he will finish off the Turks!"

With no further mishaps, they reached the city of Genoa.

The proud procession made its way straight across the land of Italy. In front marched musicians. Following them were two lance-bearers, a giant and a dwarf. Then came the two native keepers with the elephant, on which sat Prince Max, waving proudly to the onlookers on every side. Behind came the attendants with the baggage. And last of all, on two mules, followed a litter carrying Princess Maria.

Wherever the procession went, people came running from all over to see the newlyweds, Princess Maria and Prince Max.

But they forgot all about the princess and the prince as soon as they saw the gigantic, wondrous beast. They stared and marveled.

"Indeed, you may marvel, good people," a herald would cry. "You are looking at Suleiman, the renowned elephant who will free Vienna from the Turks. And his appetite is as large as he is. Bring him something to eat, or he may grow dangerous."

The people would run quickly and bring what they had, and the elephant gulped it all down. His keepers made sure that he didn't ruin his stomach.

"Thank you," Max would say graciously, and they would go on. No one bothered about Maria in the litter.

At the foot of the Alps lay the wealthy city of Trient. When the townfolk learned that the prince was bringing a monster with him, they planned a surprise. They erected a wooden framework and constructed an outline of the fabulous beast on it. Then they attached fireworks all along the outline. When night fell, the fireworks were set off, and a shining, sparkling elephant appeared in the night sky.

A bit farther on in the Tyrol lay the beautiful city of Bozen. The people there were angry because King Ferdinand neglected them. They planned not to watch when Prince Max came along with his procession.

But then they caught sight of the elephant, who almost got stuck in the narrow streets. They didn't stay in their houses after that! They brought him Tyrolean wine, which made him dance in circles in the marketplace. Max explained to the people that King Ferdinand was busy fighting the Turks, but that the elephant would soon send the Turks packing. Then the king would again have time for the Tyroleans. That made sense to the people of Bozen, and they bade a friendly goodbye to the procession.

Now the journey grew difficult. The valley was narrow, and rocks barred the way. "Take care of Suleiman!" Max called down from his seat high on the elephant.

Everyone took care, but there was an accident all the same. The elephant lost his footing and fell. If the rocks hadn't stopped him, he would have drowned in the wild mountain stream, and Max would have drowned with him.

Everyone set to work to rescue the giant animal. It took hours to raise him. Afterward they were all so exhausted they could hardly go on.

In Brixen they found an inn with a large stable. It was big enough to shelter all of them, and here they could rest at last.

During the night Max and the elephant began to run a high fever. They had caught cold when they fell into the icy water. Maria sent for the doctor. Although he knew nothing at all about elephants, he prescribed two weeks of rest, hot compresses, and lots of hot tea for the patients.

Maria tended the two of them tirelessly day and night, humming Spanish songs as she worked. Max watched her, and he liked her better and better.

As he began to get well, Max grew restless. "We must go on," he said. "Otherwise winter will surprise us before we are over the mountains."

He didn't know that winter had already arrived.

The innkeeper at Brixen had spread the news that an enormous, fabulous animal was in his stable. People poured down from the mountains and up from the valleys to see it. They were allowed to peek at the elephant secretly, and the clever innkeeper made them pay for the privilege. He was very sorry when his royal guests moved on.

Even when the stable had long been empty, the curious came each day and asked to see the marvelous beast. The innkeeper would describe to them how the elephant had been as big as a house, with legs like tree trunks, ears like sheets, and a nose as long and thick as a man's leg. No one believed him, so he had a painter paint a life-sized elephant on the inn wall. The picture can be seen there still. And ever since, that inn in Brixen has been called The Elephant.

The road led up the rocky wall to the pass. The mountains round about were dark and threatening. The wind blew icily. Snow swirled in the air.

Maria no longer sat in the litter. All wrapped up, she perched high on the elephant. "You'll be safer there," Max said, "and I can look after you." He himself carefully led the animal up the mountain. Once, when he looked back, he saw they were almost all alone. Only a few brave fellows were still following. All the others had turned back in fear.

Finally they reached the other side of the pass. They were tired, hungry, and numb with cold. The elephant was so weak that he was stumbling.

They came to a lonely mountain village. All the windows and doors were barred. Max knocked at one and begged, "At least give our elephant something to eat. Otherwise he will starve to death."

The door opened, and a woman leaned out, screaming, "That big monster would eat up all our winter provisions. Then *we'd* starve to death!" And she slammed the door in Max's face.

At evening they knocked at the door of a farmhouse where two old people lived. "Husband!" the woman exclaimed. "I think the Holy Family is outside."

She quickly dished up some soup. The man brought some hay for the elephant. They all had a warm place to spend the night.

The next day the old woman tidied up their things. Max and Maria sat there and said to each other, "I like you."

But they had to fare farther. Suleiman the elephant still had to drive away the Turks, and Max was anxious to be off. Maria gave the old woman a gold coin.

When the travelers had gone, the old people looked carefully at the gold piece. On one side were the arms of Spain and Austria. On the other were the heads of Max and Maria. "That wasn't the Holy Family, husband," said the old woman. "We have had royal guests."

In the city of Innsbruck, Max and Maria were eagerly expected. There, too, the people marveled at the elephant and brought him tidbits, but Max and Maria saw with concern that he ate nothing. Luckily the journey would be easier now. They would go on to Vienna by water.

King Ferdinand and the Viennese had been waiting for hours before the gates of the city. Finally Prince Max and Princess Maria rode toward them on the elephant.

"Long live the bride and groom!" cried the Viennese excitedly. They were happy to see how much Max and Maria loved each other. "Long live the bride and groom!"

Max raised his hand and announced: "My dear people of Vienna, we have brought you a present—this elephant here. He is called Suleiman, like the fierce leader of the Turks. He will drive the Turks away, and finally we will have peace."

Then King Ferdinand raised his hand and answered, "Dear Max, dear Maria, the Viennese have a present for you, too. They have already driven off the Turks by themselves! But they rejoice that now there is a real elephant in Vienna."

Everyone pressed forward to look at the wonderful animal more closely. Very brave people even touched him. In the press of the crowd, a woman's little son slipped out of her arms. She screamed in terror, for she was sure that the elephant would trample him. But Suleiman fished up the little boy with his trunk and handed him back to his mother.

At that, the crowd went wild. "Three cheers for the good elephant Suleiman!" the Viennese cried with one voice. "Hurrah, hurrah, hurrah!"

Max and Maria moved into a small wooden castle outside of Vienna. It is called Schoenbrunn. Suleiman the elephant lived nearby in the castle park. He was cherished and looked after and received the very best fodder. But despite all that anyone could do, he never recovered. He remained weak and ailing. Perhaps he was pining with loneliness and homesickness for his warm homeland far away.

Finally he weighed barely five hundred pounds. After two years, he died.

Max later became Emperor Maximilian the Second. Maria became empress. As the years passed, they had sixteen children.

The king of Portugal sent each new baby another strange animal as a baptismal present. Sometimes the animal came from Africa, sometimes from India. He sent a lion, a panther, a giraffe, a dromedary, a bird of paradise, and many other animals, but he never sent another elephant.

The Viennese were allowed to come into the park with their children and look at the animals. And they are still coming, for today there is a zoo in the park at Schoenbrunn.

This is what really happened:

Pages 4-5: Emperor Charles V ruled the Holy Roman Empire of the German peoples from 1519 to 1556. He betrothed his daughter Maria to Maximilian, the son of his brother Ferdinand I, king of Austria and Hungary.

Maria was prim and not especially pretty. In his youth Max was frivolous, witty, and charming.

Pages 6-7: Sultan Suleiman (or Solyman) II conquered Belgrade, then Hungary. In 1529, with an army of 120,000 Turks, he laid siege to the city of Vienna—in vain.

Pages 10-11: At that time Portugal was a great colonial power. King John III possessed an animal park with lions, tigers, panthers, leopards, giraffes, dromedaries, and birds of paradise. When he gave Max the elephant, he wrote, "My dear prince, I hope you will like this keepsake." The elephant probably came from Goa or Malacca.

Page 12: The king of Portugal had the idea of naming the elephant Suleiman. He wrote, "I think you should give the animal a new name, and that it should be the name of the mortal enemy of your royal house, Sultan Suleiman, who would thus be suitably humiliated and would at the same time become your slave."

Page 14: In those days, numerous pirates roamed the Mediterranean Sea and captured ships coming from the Orient and the Americas laden with treasure. Many of the pirates were Muslims loyal to Sultan Suleiman. When the ships in which Max, Maria, and the elephant were traveling were attacked, Maria's wardrobe was in fact lost.

Pages 16-17: The procession with the elephant went from Genoa through Liguria, Lombardy, Verona, and the Tyrol, to the Brenner Pass. How the procession must have looked can be seen in the great mural in Brixen (Bressanone). There in the picture are the two keepers and the two lance-bearers, one a giant and the other a dwarf. Unusual-looking people used to be welcomed at royal courts.

Page 19: The fireworks display at Trient (Trento) took place the night before the royal procession moved on. There had been enough time beforehand to make a wooden likeness of the elephant.

In Bozen (Bolzano) the legislature was called together and a set of demands drawn up to send to King Ferdinand through Max. The reception there was not so lavish as elsewhere. The chronicles report that people considered royal visits, with all their expensive splendor, to be plagues on the land.

Page 21: In Brixen the elephant was allowed to rest for two weeks. He was stabled in a barn beside The Inn at the High Field.

Not only in Brixen did the landlord rename his inn. There also are—or were—inns named The Elephant in Rovereto, Trento, Bozen, Auer (Ora), Sand bei Taufers, Bruneck (Brunico), Sterzing (Vipiteno), Innsbruck, Hall in Tyrol, Salzburg, Linz, Graz, and Stein on the Danube.

Page 26: After the reception in Innsbruck on January 6, the elephant traveled from Hall to Wasserburg by ship along small rivers to the Danube.

Page 28: The elephant took part in a great procession to honor the young couple. The episode with the mother who lost her child occurred during the celebration. In gratitude, the father, a well-to-do merchant, had a relief of the elephant mounted on his house.

Page 30: The records of the menagerie at Schoenbrunn state: Indian bull—Spain: Arrived March 6, 1552; died December 18, 1553.

The elephant was stuffed. Later it was presented to a Bavarian duke who was a collector of curiosities. The stuffed elephant remained in existence until 1941. It became moldy in a damp cellar where it had been stored to protect it from bombs during World War II. In an institution in Kremsmuenster there is still a chair that was made from the bones of its right foreleg.

Page 31: Prince Max became Emperor Maximilian II (1564–1576). He and Empress Maria really did have sixteen children.

Maximilian made a treaty with Suleiman's successor, after which the Turks remained peaceful for a while in return for a yearly payment of tribute. Finally the Turks were driven away altogether, but much later, in 1683.

Translator's note: At the time when Max and Maria made their long journey, the Tyrol was part of Austria. The people spoke German, and all the towns had German names. After World War I, the Tyrol became part of Italy, and the names of the towns were changed to Italian ones. Modern maps will show you the Italian names; sometimes the German ones will be given too—but sometimes not. We've given some of the Italian names in parentheses in case you'd like to trace Max and Maria's path.